There Are Cracks in My Wall

Artwork by Glenn Rodriguez

There Are Cracks in My Wall

Reconstructing the Foundations of Your Walls with a Strong Framework

Michael Turner

Tampa, Florida

The content associated with this book is the sole work and responsibility of the author. Gatekeeper Press had no involvement in the generation of this content.

There Are Cracks in My Wall: Reconstructing the Foundations of Your Walls with a Strong Framework

Published by Gatekeeper Press
7853 Gunn Hwy., Suite 209
Tampa, FL 33626
www.GatekeeperPress.com

Copyright © 2024 by Michael Turner
All rights reserved. Neither this book, nor any parts within it may be sold or reproduced in any form or by any electronic or mechanical means, including information storage and retrieval systems, without permission in writing from the author. The only exception is by a reviewer, who may quote short excerpts in a review.

The cover design for this book are entirely the product of the author. Gatekeeper Press did not participate in and is not responsible for any aspect of these elements.

Library of Congress Control Number: 2024935740

ISBN (paperback): 9781662950483

Dedication

This book honors the men who have provided guidance, counsel, and support as I have advanced on my spiritual path after the passing of my father. I am grateful for the unwavering love and support of those who have stood by me as I pursue a deeper connection to the Christian faith. This has introduced me to exceptionally knowledgeable educators who have been blessed by the Lord to guide me in deepening my understanding of the Holy Spirit. Jesus Christ is the focal point and most significant figure, radiating with brilliance and demonstrating exceptional virtues and empowerment, ultimately motivating others to strengthen their faith.

Table of Contents

Preface viii
Introduction xi

Chapter 1	There Are Cracks in My Wall 1
Chapter 2	Wholeness in the EYE 8
Chapter 3	Wholeness in Your Image 12
Chapter 4	How Can You Stand Up Against Society's Wave of Temptation? 16
Chapter 5	Examine Your Thought Life Frequently 20
Chapter 6	There Is Groundwork for Every Single One of Your Problems 22
Chapter 7	Brokenness in Thoughts 25
Chapter 8	Spiritual Brokenness 30
Chapter 9	Pray 34

Dictionary Oxford Languages 36
Author's Bio 79

Preface

My first publication about understanding the life of brokenness was when I began looking at my life as missing open doors and incomplete tasks. I quickly began taking extensive notes on my life to change from the old me to the new me by starting to draw nearer to the breaking points, where there were no wins in my life of brokenness. But in the faith realm of the Kingdom of God, His words state we win in the battle over our enemies. Like Psalms 108:13 says, "With God's help we will do mighty things, for he will trample down our foes." But only when we surrender to the defined art of the King who created us, established us, inherited us, and freed us.

The Scriptures declare God wins and reigns over our lives. The primary obstacle of brokenness must be overcome for us to understand our brokenness. In Philippians 3:12-14, what is it that made Paul such an outstanding winner? Paul makes every effort to take hold of that goal because Christ has taken hold of him. I find that it is better to meditate on one problem in which your spirit man guides you and focus on it until your breakthrough comes.

Introduction

I see many Christian men in the church who would like to walk in the wholeness of Christ, but they struggle and will not open up on the issue of life. They think, why I should tell my business to someone who may be broken themselves too? Fellow men, it's important to acknowledge that we all have our flaws and struggles, whether it be lying, stealing, cheating, engaging in unhealthy sexual behaviors, or other forms of deceit and manipulation. So, ask yourself, where do I fit in? I can recall asking a friend to hold me accountable for my life issues. I can tell you it is an eye-opener having two men helping each other with one accord.

I am asking you to check the boundaries in which you are stopping the living flow of God's healing for you. Ask yourself if you can find someone in your place of influence and tell them your problem so they can come together with you and help you to overcome the issue. We have many men who can pray with breakthrough prayers and still build their character in Christ Jesus, hold you accountable, chastise you to see the enemy's plan for you, and indicate the faults with bold statements to your patterns. Think about how you are valuable to the Kingdom of God with great insight, foresight, wisdom, courage, and fear. What a great substance you have in stored in your inner man is the Holy Spirit. You are the image of Christ built up with superb attributes that are hungry for the Kingdom of God (Romans 14:17 NIV).

Happiness is something you can cultivate and practice in simple ways every day. Every day, a new breath you take brings a unique opportunity to open your heart and mind to become whole in him without fault; it embraces the true character of Christ in you; it fills all broken and cracked walls. God created you with great love, power, a sound mind, and the opportunity to step into a new level of wholeness.

Individuals with disabilities possess a remarkable level of craftsmanship, often overlooked and marginalized by society. Despite these societal barriers, they can create exceptional and high-quality work. Artwork by Glenn Rodriguez

CHAPTER 1

There Are Cracks in My Wall

We all understand the word brokenness; it is a state of strong emotional pain that stops someone from living a normal or healthy life, as Cambridge English Dictionary defines it. The Spiritual real of God is described as a state of self-imposed fragmentation by disregarding God's truth and not obeying it. This is like David after his affair with Bathsheba (Psalm 52). It's painful to face our true selves, capable of terrible things.

No one gets through life without feeling the brokenness of this world. If you've ever gotten an unpleasant phone call, endured a serious physical affliction, or lost somebody you cherish, you know what I'm talking about. And if you have not yet experienced a life circumstance that brings you to your knees, one day you may. Don't let that reality alarm you. Let it calm you and coordinate your being to look to Jesus, the One who overcomes the world and who has created the world in his will for healing.

As we explore the word of wholeness, it gives us the state of being unbroken or undamaged. We can't navigate this world by ourselves; if we could, I think we all would be in a new realm of growth because we would grasp an understanding of the process of wholeness within our thoughts and would experience a transition to self-dependence and self-government. Our opinions and beliefs are about ourselves, along with others and the world around us.

Our thoughts can be experienced in all different ways. Some of us think in words, some in pictures, and some in both. We tell ourselves that we are okay, but in reality, we are broken and beaten down. We think that we are on the right path because God has opened a door for us. We believe that we are being healed from our past hurts, but God says that we need to work on the pain that we have been carrying around for so long. This is a step toward wholeness. So, we stand on a scaffold with a safety harness to protect us from falling, not understanding this safety harness has a short range in how far we can go.

I remember the rejection I felt when I was twelve. I used to ask my father to take me to baseball games. One day, I received a free ticket, but my father couldn't take me because he had to work. I felt rejected and stopped asking him to take me to games. This pattern continued, and I began to feel worthless and insignificant. My low self-esteem prevented me from having a relationship with my father.

We can see a pattern of damage in my life. To begin the process of healing, we must acknowledge the basics of our pain and suffering. One day, I was in church when God spoke to me. He said, "Give me your father." I was confused and asked, "What should I do?" God instructed me to place both of my hands on my heart and lift them up to Him. I followed His instructions and immediately broke down crying because my feelings toward my father had changed. God then opened the door for me to attend two baseball games for free. I invited my father to join me, and we had great seats right on the first base line. The day after the games, I asked God what had happened during this process. He revealed that my grandfather had died when my father was only twelve years old. This event had taught my father how to become a young man. Through this experience, I can see a pattern of brokenness in my life.

Let's return to the wholeness of God. He said we can do all things through Christ Jesus, who strengthens us. Our own process can't accomplish this because we have been damaged in so many ways until we have lost focus on what is true in life. God would like for us to return to the foundation of His wholeness, which He gave us at the beginning of life. Frequently, individuals construct their self-concept based on material possessions and external perceptions, overlooking the significance of self-awareness. We starve our inner man with deadly words. We should feed our inner man with positive things, ideas, and great concepts so we can work it, feed it, or live it out. Remember, God looks at the inner man, and the world looks at the outer man.

God's original design for man was to be whole, which means being effectively well in body, soul, and spirit. This can also be broken down into mind, will, and emotions. This was God's original design for man before the fall of Adam and Eve and is now attainable once we join Jesus in Heaven. God created a physical body from the earth's soil and breathed life into it. The human body came alive with a spirit that gave life to man, and it became a living soul. From that point forward, humans have had a spiritual nature with a soul within a physical body.

Each part of the human body is unpredictable, yet they are joined together in a marvelous way. This makes the human body a masterpiece of God's workmanship (Ephesians 2:10). Just as the body is made up of numerous parts, so too is the entirety of the self created to operate as a total unit (1 Corinthians 12:12). After being born into the physical realm, our souls become exposed to various detrimental outcomes that originate from the pervasive presence of sin in the world. Additionally, our individual transgressions and morally unacceptable behaviors have a harmful influence on our emotional, cognitive, and physiological states of well-being.

So you see, we are broken in several ways, and we are hidden behind many things. We think life can't see us hurting from our brokenness on this platform. In my case, I am hidden behind a scaffold structure, hoping no one can see me. I am on borrowed time because this structure is only temporary. My eye sees it differently because my mind, soul, and body are wounded and unhealthy. I need God to start breaking down the scaffold so I can be exposed and understand what is going on.

God is telling me that it is time for restoration and healing in the mind, soul, and body. They require an overhaul. It is through the work of the Holy Spirit within me that we have an opportunity to progress in our souls toward even greater wholeness. Our polluted emotions, will, and thinking can be transformed by the renewal of our minds and by the sanctifying work of the Holy Spirit in our lives to heal the broken pieces. God will always ask you to surrender more and more of your brokenness to the Holy Spirit so that He can work in our lives.

God uses this state to cleanse us, or set us aside for an extraordinary purpose. This process can transform us or restore us daily so that we become more like Jesus. 2 Corinthians 3:18 NLT says, "So all of us who have had that veil removed can see and reflect the glory of the Lord. And the Lord—who is the Spirit—makes us more and more like him as we are changed into his glorious image."

Our responsibility is to purify ourselves from all defilement of flesh and spirit, perfecting holiness in the fear of God (2 Corinthians 7:1 ASV). We are encouraged to take an active role in "stripping off all that restrains us" (Hebrews 12:1) so that we can better shine in the full image of Christ.

The state of our bodies can vary in terms of physical health, well-being, and overall completeness. Despite outward appearances of good health, underlying circumstance may not be flawless. It is safe to assume that we do not always exhibit completely healthy behaviors. To be whole, we need to operate in a way that reflects that wholeness. This means giving up the sexual nakedness of the spiritual image we pick up over time in our lives. We must strive to see wholeness, which means overcoming the brokenness of our true vision to be whole, along with our strength, and set our minds back in order. We must see, fight, and conquer this spiritual battle for wholeness. In Genesis

1:27, God said He created man in His image. In the image of God, He created him, male and female. He created them. This is a spiritual connection.

The enemy always wants to change our image, so he uses this battle tactic to create a change. When we connect sexually with someone or something perverted, we begin to change the great picture we were created to be. We pick up people's habits and bond with another spirit. Look at the things you may not be in your bloodline, and suddenly, you manifest it in your life; this pattern is connected to soul ties and to the people you have bonded with sexually. To break this pattern, we need to dismiss all of these things (Romans 1:7). The perverted twisted into a reprobate mind pattern as God gave them over in the lusts of their hearts to impurity so that their bodies would be dishonored among them (verse 24, NASB). God gave them over to a depraved mind to do those things which are not proper (verse 28, NASB), and the enemy is cloning a perverted image of his Kingdom in use.

When we want to be free, we can ask the Holy Spirit for direction. In my case, I ask the Holy Spirit to bring back all of the images that are connected to me so that I can dismiss these images by saying, "In the name of Jesus, I rebuke you." After that, I plead the blood of Jesus over myself and my mind. It is important to remember that the enemy has no right to invade us unless we open the door for him to come in. This process may take a while because the enemy may hire someone or something to make us forget about the image, and he can use this battle tactic to enter into our thought pattern. We must close all open vessels that relate to the world system in us. I encourage you to be patient and let the Holy Spirit guide you. As it says in John 16:13, "But when he, the Spirit of truth, comes, he will guide you into all the truth. He will not speak on his own; he will speak only what he hears, and he will tell you what is yet to come."

CHAPTER **2**

Wholeness in the EYE

Jesus said, "The eye is the lamp of the body. If your eyes are good, your whole body will be full of light" (Matthew 6:22). Here, our Lord describes the eye as a lamp that lights the entire body. Our eyes are the entrance to our hearts and minds, and as such, they provide a doorway to our very souls.

Our eyes can be utilized to see what is good or evil, what is helpful or hurtful, and the things we see influence our whole being. If we see goodness, that will transmit outward from inside our hearts and minds. But if we permit our eyes to wait on wickedness, we are so influenced by what we see that darkness begins to exude from inside and can corrupt us and those around us.

The Bible says Satan pretends to be an angel of light. That's his extraordinary deception—to make individuals think they've found the light when, in fact, it's the darkness of fabricated light (2 Corinthians 11:14). His purpose is to dazzle us to truth and pervert our minds. He uses our eyes to gain access to our hearts. He parades before us all kinds of evil, from the downpour of pornography on the internet to the inundation of worldly products that appeal to our materialistic driving forces.

He cheats us into accepting that these things will make us cheerful, satisfied people when they all exploit us for the joy we long for. He wants us to permit increasing darkness into our minds through the books we flick through, the images we watch, and the pictures we allow our eyes to engage in. In that way, the light of the glory of God sparkling within the light of our Lord Jesus Christ is obscured to us. Even though the light is all over—just like the afternoon sun beaming down on the earthly rim, a blinding light—if our eyes are ceaselessly centering on sin, the light we see is no light. If we need to be filled with the genuine light, we must be turned from sin, atone, and ask God to excuse us, cleanse us, and open our spiritual eyes. At that point, we must commit to being cautious about what we permit our eyes to engage. We protect our hearts and souls by guarding our eyes' gates.

Were we to take a snapshot of things in our eye gate the right way, it would store this image in the heart compartment like a Rolodex. It's on our hard drive, and the enemy can access this image at any time because he has access code to get in so he can pull us into an impure state with twisted images. He makes it look okay to see by pulling us deeper into the dark hole where we fall into the pit further. As you let sinful things enter the eye gate, you can become unresponsive in seeing what your anointed eye should see. Remember God resides in you like Romans 8:11 states, and if the Spirit of him who raised Jesus from the dead is living in you, he who raised Christ from the dead will also give life to your mortal bodies because of Christ Spirit who lives in you.

This spiritual ignorance is similar to the people's unrealistic hopes in Christ's time. Still, there is one significant difference: the individuals belonging to His church can connect with His Spirit—His thoughts, His emotions, his viewpoint—and therefore should be less hindered by the ignorance that affects worldly individuals.

When your eyes are anointed with eye salve, which is called healing for the eye in Revelation 3:18 NIV, you have the means to see more clearly. Christians have access to a more accurate lens, which is why the author of Revelation says, "Anoint your eyes with eye salve, that you may see." As Revelation states, individuals bear the responsibility of enhancing their perception, for it is God's Spirit that resides within us. This assistance helps us overcome the initial deficiency of knowledge among Christ's disciples.

Great Scripture gives two related standards concerning otherworldly vision, especially being able to approximately see God—and as we see God more clearly, our recognition of all supernatural things will improve. To begin with, Jesus tells us that the pure in heart—those without cunning, pride, lip service, envy, jealousy, competition, covered-up outrage, double-mindedness, or any other defilement or inward sin—will see God (Matthew 5:8). Within the same vein, Hebrews 12:14 says that without holiness—God's consecration of us combined with our submission to His prerequisites for moral purity—one will not see God. Our spiritual vision will be as great as our purity of intellect and conduct. Any defilement will influence our spiritual sight, making it a never-ending challenge to see things as God sees them.

As before, your journey amplifies your wholeness in your relationship with God. God looks for us to talk to him daily, along with our faith connection, in bringing wholeness to our eyesight. Our insight gave us an unmistakable picture of how it operates, which opened up our understanding of how to see the enemy at work in our life; you can strategize on how to overcome this issue. The goal is to be set free. Remember, wholeness is freedom from all things that are holding you captive. Our wholeness is the inner healing in which we open up to our believer's wisdom, love, impartation, and encouragement.

Matthew 13:16-17: "But you have God-blessed eyes—eyes that see! And God-blessed ears—ears that hear." A lot of people, prophets and humble believers among them, would have given anything to know what you are seeing, to hear what you are hearing, but never had the chance.

CHAPTER **3**

Wholeness in Your Image

Purity means the quality or state of being free from mixture, pollution, or other foreign elements. The term "purity" may refer to things such as gold (Exodus 25:17) and oil (Leviticus 24:2). In this case, we will use the term "people" to reach our mark of purity in Christ Jesus. I think that the word "character" is a good way to understand that we are made in the image of Christ, who is pure, righteous, and holy. In keeping yourself pure, you need to remember you are in a battle and all kinds of elements will come your way to pull you in a different direction so you will not see or think Christlike; if you accept this mission, you will because a perfect target for the enemy.

Ask yourself these critical questions:

- **What images, people, or places are you likely to encounter today that might encourage you to think impure thoughts?**
- **How will you prepare yourself to respond to these temptations?**

In purity, work has several great-built characters. It is a disciplined lifestyle that gives you more control. The more disciplined you become, the more you can take control over your life (which is far better than letting your life take control over you).

Proverbs 23:12 advises us to "Commit yourself to instruction and listen carefully to words of knowledge." It taught us three things. First, it said to [c]ommit yourself to instruction, so something is coming for you. Second, listen carefully to the awareness of information and skills acquired by a person. 2 Peter 1:5–6 teaches us to make every effort to supplement our faith with goodness, goodness with knowledge, knowledge with self-control, self-control with endurance, endurance with godliness. Thus, God's word is clear: we must exercise self-discipline in all matters. And as we build a character of purity with self-discipline, we become one in Christ. We must look at our lives and how God sees us in all of the pure thought. Along with pure thoughts, pure image, and what we hearing while walking the Word out. 1 Corinthians 9:27 says, "But I keep under my body and bring it into subjection: lest that by any means, when I have preached to others, I myself should be a castaway." (Meaning, check yourself.) Our significant accomplishments usually require work, perseverance, and disciplined believers to be willing to work for the rewards we so earnestly desire.

We can think about something like being unclean and having no danger, but being clean causes us to be attacked with all kinds of thoughts, images, and impure words to pull us away from God alone. We should focus our thoughts on the Word. Like in Philippians 4:8, "whatever is true, whatever is honorable, whatever is just, whatever is pure, whatever is lovely, whatever is commendable, if there is any excellence, if there is anything worthy of praise, think about these things."

How can a young man keep his way pure as in Psalm 119:9? What is the secret of living a pure life? We are living according to God's Word. Also, choose friends who love the Lord and have pure hearts. Avoid anything that leads you to have impure thoughts, especially those that are common among young men. Instead, focus on doing what is right, having faith, showing love, and seeking peace. Do this with others who also follow the Lord with a pure heart.

When you fall in love, it's natural to want to express your love in physical ways. But you also know God wants you to remain pure—in both your actions and your thoughts. This can be tough for some, but remember, your thoughts must be in a place of righteousness. And you need to respect the other person's physical ways. Rather than making the innocent expressions a mere prelude to the "heavier stuff," make the most of them. This expression of tenderness by simply putting your arms around each other means something. Or make sure a kiss communicates true feelings and isn't just the first step to further physical involvement. You need to pace your passion. If you are a runner in a marathon, you don't use your energy at the beginning of the race. You need most of it at the end, when it will bring the most value to the package you are looking for on your wedding day.

Pacing yourself means realizing you're trying to remain pure at all costs. The package you see at the door doesn't mean you touch it or someone will take it, someone will steal it from you. This means you respect what is before you and value your life. Life is an economic value used to quantify the benefit of avoiding mortality. We want to avoid igniting the fire of passion prematurely, as this may cause us to pursue a relationship that is not yet ready to move forward into the unity of oneness. Remember whose property you're touching; you do not own the person. That person belongs to God.

The image is not for use to feed your fantasies with lustful advancement or explicit sexual thoughts. We need to choose our entertainment carefully, like the books we read and the pictures we watch. They open the door for a wrong activity to come in and change the image that you were created to be. If you had one word to say before you died, would it be a word of repentance or a great lie?

CHAPTER **4**

How Can You Stand Up Against Society's Wave of Temptation?

By learning to direct your thoughts and eye in ways pleasing to God almighty . . . and by relying upon Him to deliver you from the evils that threaten you. In all of your temptations, God has promised that, with his help, you can resist every thought and image that confronts you.

In all of this, in fighting Satan, you are never alone. God is always with you, and a good starting point on your end is simply learning to recognize the subtle temptations surrounding you. The images of immorality are ubiquitous, and the enemy intends to take over your mind, heart, vision, purse, life, and, most of all, your soul. Don't let them do it.

We forget about the power of our Father in heaven. God tells us that 'if you have faith as small as a mustard seed, you can say to this mountain, move from here to there, and it will move' (Matthew 17:20 NIV). So why can't we believe he will remove the image that fueled our thoughts? Did you know that, in nearly every book of the New Testament, we're commanded to avoid sexual impurity? Let's go to the source that will help us: what the Bible teaches about sexual conduct.

According to the Scriptures in 1 Thessalonians 4: 3–5, it is generally the will of God for individuals to engage in acts of purification, specifically abstaining from indulging in sexual immorality. Each individual is expected to possess the knowledge and skill to maintain their physical body in a state of sanctified blessing and honor. It is important that these actions are not motivated by trivial matters.

Lustful desires are commonly observed among non-believers who are unaware of the divine principles taught by God. 1 Thessalonians 4: 3–5 suggests that people have a natural tendency to purify themselves, especially by avoiding sexual immorality. It is expected that all individuals should have the necessary knowledge and skills to maintain their physical well-being with virtuous dedication and respect. It is crucial to understand that these behaviors should not be guided only by biological urges, as is often observed in individuals who lack faith and are oblivious to the divine teachings provided by God.

The above claim introduces a divided clarification that should be shared with individuals, encompassing accuracy. It is suggested that people refrain from associating with individuals who assert they have a specific identity. The individual identified as Christian is found to engage in sexual transgressions. As echoed, it is strongly advised to refrain from partaking in a relationship with an individual of such character.

1 Corinthians 6:18 NIV tells us to flee sexual immorality! "Every sin that a man does is outside the body, but he who commits sexual immorality sins against his own body." This is

what 1 Corinthians 6:18 states, and Romans 12:1–2 brings a mind-changing message: "I beseech you, therefore, brothers, by the mercies of God, that you present your bodies a living sacrifice, Holy, acceptable to God, which is your reasonable service. And be not conformed to this world: but be you transformed by the renewing of your mind that you may prove; what is that good, and acceptable, and perfect, will of God." We are guided only by physical urges, as is often observed in individuals who lack faith and are oblivious to the divine teachings provided by God.

The statement above provides a clear explanation that should be communicated to people with precision. It is suggested that individuals refrain from associating with individuals who assert they have a certain identity. The individual identified as Christian is found to engage in sexual transgressions. It is highly advised to refrain from having a meal with someone of that kind of reputation, as has been consistently mentioned.

In my discovery, we are enticed in a number of ways to draw us out of the cover of Christ. A few of the ways we become trapped are when we:

- are in difficult times of life
- have an undisciplined thought life
- give in to the sexual temptation and feel alone
- live in separation from other men!
- accept the myth of materialism
- let loose with our tongues in outrage
- compare ourselves to and judge others

Let's Talk About It: Temptation

"It starts all in the great battle ground of the mind."

James 1:14-15: When a person is carried away with desire, lured by lust, and when desire becomes the focus and takes control, it gives birth to sin. When sin becomes fully grown, it produces death.

We need to understand the origin of temptation and realize that God isn't the one who tempts you. Remember to commit to controlling your thought life before it controls you.

As You Read James 1:13-14:

- Have you ever blamed God for your struggles with temptation? Why or why not?
- Think about this: if God is not author of temptation, then how does He use it in our lives? Read Matthew 6:13; 1 Corinthians 10:13.
- How does lust carry us away and entice us? What is your experience with this?

CHAPTER 5

Examine Your Thought Life Frequently

Once righteousness is attained, along with faith, love, and peace, one must surround oneself with those who wholeheartedly invoke the Lord. Do not let love transform into desire, leading to a negative path of excessive sexual activity, disrespectful behaviors, or selfish greed. You will receive this adorned cloak as a visual symbol of the LORD's commands, reminding you to obey them and resist the temptations of your heart and eyes. God has summoned us to lead lives of holiness rather than impurity. As a result, those who reject these rules are not simply disregarding human teachings but instead defying God, who bestows His Holy Spirit upon you. Anything that exists in this world, including desires for physical pleasure, material possessions, and arrogant behavior, does not originate from a divine source but is influenced by the world.

Your thought is a form of spiritual integrity. I like James 1:2–4, which says, "Dear brothers and sisters, when troubles of any kind come your way, consider it an opportunity for great joy. For you know that when your faith is tested, your endurance has a chance to grow. So let it grow, for when your endurance is fully developed, you will be perfect and complete, needing nothing." God would like his son to have goals for growth in the myth of your test, to build his character, understand how to stand firm in these trials, and commit to praying instead of complaining and collapsing.

Let's Talk About It: Spiritual Integrity Thought in Reading James 1:1–12:

- What kinds of trials do you think James is referring to in this passage?
- Why do you think he exhorts us to respond with a joyful heart during times of testing and trial?
- What do you think a joyful heart looks like in the midst of a trial?
- How does testing faith produce endurance?
- What are a few destructive ways that you think? How can you change your reaction?

CHAPTER **6**

There Is Groundwork for Every Single One of Your Problems

Think about those things in your life that you've always just written off as character flaws or just a part of who you are. It does not matter the problem or flaw in your character; you can have a number of these things: anxiety, fear, depression, addictions, sins, and bad habits. Yes, they, too, have a name, but whose names have the power to uplift and destroy all of the enemy's dysfunctional solutions he imposes on us to change our character, beliefs, and make us second guess our true character? Proverbs 7:3 states that Solomon encourages his son to keep the lessons he is learning close to his heart and mind. It is expected to tell people to "tie a string around your finger," as a reminder of something. The things we call dark, inflicted issues have something to answer to; they indicate weakness when we agree to demands or follow orders from authority.

I can't stress enough who is above all names, and He is the authority who operates under the crown ship of the highest God. His name is Jesus.

Nowadays, you find people everywhere you look with spiritual hindrances they've taken on as part of their identity.

But I want to compel you today to look at every part of your being—even those tricky things that have become a part of who you are and have been there your whole life—and challenge yourself to fight against them with God's help and His Word.

I don't want to minimize the impact of mental illness or trauma, but I'm here to offer hope. There is a living God who can provide a cure for everything. What the world says is incurable, the power of the living God healed. You must believe it, accept it, walk in it, and follow it wholeheartedly to experience the fullness of this power in your life.

Read Psalm 103:1–5 on a daily basis to help build you up: "Bless the Lord, O my soul; and all that is within me, bless His Holy name!, Bless the Lord, O my soul, and forget not all His benefits: Who forgives all your iniquities, Who heals all your diseases, Who redeems your life from destruction, Who crowns you with loving-kindness and tender mercies, Who satisfies your mouth with good things, So that your youth is renewed like the eagle?"

There Are Cracks in My Wall

Artwork by Glenn Rodriguez

CHAPTER **7**

Brokenness in Thoughts

Feeling broken usually means that you feel like there's something you don't know how to change but want to. There are generally additional words or thought patterns that can help you get a fuller picture of what's going on and how to address it. The Merriam-Webster dictionary states that intense emotional pain stops someone from living an everyday or healthy life: can we acknowledge our brokenness and look for great healing? Brokenness is being unfruitful in the things of God, and it breaks down the heart in our belief system, faith pattern, strategies we can create, the insight of our vision, and the foresight of the eye. As you see this pattern of destruction in your thoughts, you need to address your thoughts.

This can be very painful because you are trying to think about the wholesome life you want in Christ. But the enemy is still attacking your mind with polluted thoughts along with action. Do not think the enemy plays fair. Your mind is the battleground. He works daily to change your thoughts. He brings up all kinds of old patterns to make you think of the good times you had in the world's system, in which he checks to see if he can activate your flesh in the power of lustful thought patterns. Remember, the enemy's seed also creates the fruit of darkness. God planted on the earth a pattern for his people in John 12:24: "Verily, verily I say unto you, except a corn of wheat fall into the ground and die, it abides alone; but if it dies, it brings forth much fruit."

The enemy uses words to create dark times in your life and bring brokenness. I cannot stress enough the power of God's Word to remove all bad seeds from your soil and plant seeds of growth for the Kingdom of God to bring wholeness.

Our thoughts can affect our lives in many ways. If we focus on negative thoughts, they can prevent us from growing and experiencing joy, comfort, wisdom, knowledge, and understanding. This can cause pain and disrupt our sense of wholeness. It's important to focus on positive thoughts and ideas that will help us grow and improve.

1. A significant obstacle. Wisdom is the principal thing: therefore, get wisdom; "with all thy getting get understanding" (Proverbs 4:7). To become whole in God, it is important to understand your place in the world. The enemy is attacking you in the areas of your eyes, mind, and thoughts because he knows your accurate assignment.
2. Our life is more about the life of a Christian than working. Our light shines so bright it draws God's people to the light of his glory, which we demonstrate in our work by bringing healing to the mind. The Word says to call those things as though they were. Romans 4:17 focuses on speaking about things as if they already exist,

demonstrating the potency of God's promises and His steadfast determination to fulfill them.
3. The fruit we choose can overflow in our life by being united with Christ and walking in His fullness; this demonstrates God's character. God is committed to His relationship with us, so we must be devoted to Him. God will not betray your confidence; he is Holy, truthful, righteous, and just in his character, so we need to be in this attribute of the character of Christ. Remember, your light opens the eye to someone to understand his light in use.
4. It's not what I do but what I'm becoming by God's grace. We need to look at the power of God, who has to fill us up with his glory, and we will not achieve his wholeness unless we focus on the words of God daily. Our thought means renewing your mind daily and bringing the threats to the enemy and not letting the enemy threaten us. Remember the WORD; it brings life and a refresher to your mind and your Spirit.

"The word of God is Spirit and life. It is the spirit that quickeneth the flesh profiteth nothing the words that I speak unto you, they are Spirit, and they are life" (John 6:63). Additionally, according to Hebrews 4:12, when the Holy Spirit quickens an active believer, they have the dynamic power to impart spiritual life to others.

The enemy is to keep you from renewing your mind daily; the enemy has chosen to threaten you by discouragement and broken-down faith. Our weakness keeps us dependent on God's strength to engage us in a clear thought pattern with him. Accept your vulnerability, whether it's the vulnerability of your situation or what you perceive in yourself, and offer it to him. He desires his strength to be made perfect in your weakness. Rest is available when we abide in him. Be wise in your ways, present your life as a pleasing sacrifice to Him, even in the face of challenges, and you will become a vessel of His strength and majesty.

Let Break Bread in This Brokenness in Thoughts: Read: Isaiah 55:8-9 and Luke 10:19

Can you think of a time when you formed an unclean thought in your mind and did not repent? When you do not repent, it gives the enemy more access to tear you down or destroy you. This is why God gave us the Word of Faith, to stop the enemy in his tracks from attacking you.

How many times are you going to let the enemy attack you in your thoughts and your character? Stop and focus on the words and destroy the enemy. Luke 10:19 says, "Behold, I have given you authority to tread on serpents and scorpions, and over all the power of the enemy." And nothing shall by any means hurt you. You have the power of access to the upper room of grace to walk in the fullness of His glory.

A. What does "my ways are not your ways" mean?
B. Read Colossians 4:2 for further instructions.
C. Our brokenness made us open to His work in use and allowed God to really get to work in our lives.

Brokenness in Thoughts

By Glenn Rodriguez (Arts only)

CHAPTER **8**

Spiritual Brokenness

We can see brokenness in two ways, one from God's perspective, which will produce lasting transformation with us. On the other, we are in a state of spiritual brokenness and emotions that flood the past relationship. This may imply a messy life composed entirely of imperfection. It may mean being heartbroken from old things, from deep wounds of the past, leading to spiritual distress and disconnection.

That comes from recognizing the enormity of one's sins. I use this word enormity because sometimes we magnify our sin, which can devastate the mind and prevent us from seeking salvation. We must also realize that we could be affected by a design that causes dysfunction in our lives, such as enduring injury, unresolved guilt and shame, a need for purpose and meaning, or sin and insubordination. This pattern results from not feeding the spiritual man every day with the words of God. We can qualify this by His words. Here are a few examples of the brokenness that brings spiritual pollution to the intellect:

- People who have experienced past harm or betrayal may have difficulty trusting others. They may find it hard to open up or depend on individuals due to these past

experiences. As a result, they may be guarded and have a negative outlook on relationships.
- Long-term injury, abuse, or neglect can lead to a loss of self-esteem. This can cause people to doubt their abilities and value. They may engage in negative self-talk, constantly criticizing and blaming themselves.
- People who have trouble controlling their emotions may experience anger issues, uncertainty, and passionate torment. This can manifest as outrage, irritability, or even rage. Often, their anger is a cover-up for more profound feelings of sadness or harm.
- Some people who are struggling with emotional pain turn to drinking, shopping, gambling, or other addictive behaviors to try to escape their torment and fill the emptiness they feel inside. These coping mechanisms may provide temporary relief, but they can also cause more harm in the long run.
- Anxiety, panic, and depression can often manifest as feelings of inner turmoil, low self-esteem, and difficulty forming close relationships. Initiation of the healing process often requires seeking professional counseling or therapy. With empathy and assistance, people who have suffered emotional trauma can regain their self-esteem, cultivate more positive relationships, establish limits, and break free from their traumatic experiences.
- Recognizing the signs that emotional healing is necessary is the initial step. Remember that people who have been hurt and betrayed often create walls around themselves to protect themselves. Their past hardships have shown them

that being open and vulnerable only brings more suffering, so they protect themselves by shutting off their emotions. We can continue to explore the challenges of establishing boundaries, building trust, feeling undeserving of love from others and family, being apprehensive of intimacy, and carrying deep emotional wounds ingrained in our behavior.

Also, we can see brokenness in three different ways by reading three powerful stories in the Bible:

1. Brokenness through empathy–John 11. One of Jesus's dear friends, Lazarus, died. Lazarus's death was not a surprise to Christ. He knew he would soon raise Lazarus from the dead. Yet, in verse 35, the Bible tells us Jesus wept. Jesus was all-powerful but experienced brokenness because the people around him were so broken. As believers of Christ, we care for them as Christ did in John 13:34, along with Ephesians 4:32. We are all called to carry one another's burdens.
2. Brokenness through our choice of sin–King David, a man after God's heart, made some bad choices. He slept with a married woman, Bathsheba, whose husband was away at war fighting for Israel, and then he had her husband killed in battle to prevent him from finding out about their infidelity. Sometimes, we, too, choose our way. In Psalm 51, we see David broken before God over his sin. Because of David's repentant heart, the Lord restored him.

3. Brokenness through circumstances–We read in 1 Samuel 1 about Hannah and the brokenness she experienced because of infertility. Just as I didn't choose the circumstance in my own life of losing a good friend, Hannah didn't select the circumstance of infertility. But her despair brought her to a place of complete vulnerability and transparency before the Lord. She surrendered her brokenness to Him in faith, asked for a son, and chose to praise him in her pain and desperation. God answered Hannah's prayer and gave her a son.

Spiritual brokenness can lead to humbleness, surrender, repentance, and redemption through Jesus Christ. We can choose whether we will stay broken. Christ would put those broken pieces back together to restore the beautiful vessel he can use for his glory. God will not permit us to use our flesh to cope with life. He has provided a way of dealing with life, which is much better than the coping mechanism of our cycle.

Our Father, who operates in the heavenly realm, said in Romans 8:12–13 that Paul wants us to kick the flesh to the curb so that we can experience the abundant life God has promised. If we put to death the deeds of the body, we will live. We can overcome the discouragement of lousy singleness and financial stress because "he who is in us is greater than the one who is in the world" (1 John 4:4).

CHAPTER **9**

Pray

"Father, we stand in your presence. Only you know what our potential is. Please help us to die to our selfish, independent spirits. I pray for a renewed mind in the name of Jesus. I commit to repenting for my behavior. I pray for the unsaved and saved people I impact daily who have bad thoughts. I pray in Jesus's name that we would surrender all to Jesus and live every day for you. Let them hold and occupy the promise you have for them in Jesus's name."

"Lord, thank you for letting us come together on one accord with the faith covered by God's words. John 10:10 says, 'The thief comes only to steal and kill and destroy. I came that they may have life and have it abundantly.' But our wholeness is in you and the brokenness. You heal us in the presence of your glory as in Psalm 107:20: 'He sent out his word, healed them, and delivered them from their destruction.'"

"Father, you did not give us the Spirit of Fear but the Power of sound minds, and we received this in the name of Jesus. And when the enemy brings this spirit to us, we may be startled, but we will put our trust in you, Lord. Like Psalm 56:6, we are strong and courageous."

"Therefore, we do not walk in anxiety. We walk in the power of Christ, whose strength is with us because of our power and love. With self-control, we bring the light of God to show us the power we have over the enemy. We leave with peace, and we give peace to others. Not as the world gives, but as we give."

"So let not our hearts be troubled, neither let us be afraid. Because of our living conditions, we can't be scared of people; we must speak to others with boldness. Lord, you strengthen us with the power of Jesus and his Name."

Dictionary Oxford Languages

A dictionary serves as a reference tool for accessing information on the definitions, forms, pronunciation, usages, and etymologies of words, thereby contributing to the enrichment, augmentation, and enhancement of their value and improving their quality and attractiveness. I use the "Dictionary Data from Oxford Languages, Language: English Release Date: December 2002 Publisher: Oxford University Press, USA; Length: 1312 Pages, Ludinda Coventry." Also "Merriam-Webster.com Dictionary." No other dictionary matches M-W's accuracy and scholarship in defining word meanings. Our pronunciation help, synonyms, usage and grammar tips set the standard. Go beyond dictionary lookups with Word of the Day, facts and observations on language, lookup trends, and wordplay from the editors at Merriam-Webster Dictionary. © 2024 Merriam-Webster, Incorporated

A

Anoint

The symbolic act of pouring oil on objects or individuals as a sign of consecration. The name Messiah means the Anointed One.

Accomplish

To bring about (a result) by effort have much to accomplish today

To bring to completion: FULFILL accomplish a job

To succeed in reaching (a stage in a progression) would starve before accomplishing half the distance

B

Bold

fearless before danger: INTREPID bold settlers on some foreign shore—William Wordsworth

showing or requiring a fearless daring spirit a bold plan

Bloodline

A sequence of direct ancestors especially in a pedigree

Brokenness

having been fractured or damaged and no longer in one piece or in working order:

He had a broken arm

Broken Down

to cause to fall or collapse by breaking or shattering

to make ineffective break down legal barriers

to divide into parts or categories

to separate (something, such as a chemical compound) into simpler substances: DECOMPOSE

to take apart especially for storage or shipment and for later reassembling

C

Calm

a period or condition of freedom from storms, high winds, or rough activity of water a sailing ship motionless in the calm

complete absence of wind or presence of wind having a speed no greater than one mile (1.6 kilometers) per hour; see Beaufort Scale Table 2: a state of tranquility at dusk a; quiet calm settled over the town.

Cognitive

of, relating to, being, or involving conscious intellectual activity (such as thinking, reasoning, or remembering) cognitive impairment

based on or capable of being reduced to empirical factual knowledge cognitively adverb

D

Disobedience (Verb)

To make unclean or impure: such as a: to corrupt the purity or perfection of: DEBASE

E

Emotional (Adjective)

of or relating to emotion an *emotional* disorder

dominated by or prone to emotion an *emotional* person

appealing to or arousing emotion an *emotional* sermon

markedly aroused or agitated in feeling or sensibilities gets emotional at weddings emotionally adverb

Extraordinary (Adjective)

going beyond what is usual, regular, or customary extraordinary powers

exceptional to a very marked extent extraordinary beauty

of a financial transaction: NONRECURRING

employed for or sent on a special function or service;

Exude (Verb)

to ooze out

to undergo diffusion *transitive verb*

to cause to ooze or spread out in all directions

to display conspicuously or abundantly

F

Freedom (Noun)

the quality or state of being free: such as

the absence of necessity, coercion, or constraint in choice or action

liberation from slavery or restraint or from the power of another INDEPENDENCE the quality or state of being <u>exempt</u> or released usually from something onerous freedom from care

unrestricted use gave him the freedom of their home

Foundation (Noun)

the act of <u>founding</u> .There since the *foundation* of the school

a basis (such as a tenet, principle, or axiom) upon which something stands or is supported, the *foundations* of geometry; the rumor is without *foundation* in fact

funds given for the permanent support of an institution: ENDOWMENT

an organization or institution established by endowment with provision for future maintenance a trust administered by a *foundation*

G

Generation (Noun)

a body of living beings constituting a single step in the line of descent from an ancestor

a group of individuals born and living contemporaneously the younger generation

a group of individuals having contemporaneously a status (such as that of students in a school) which each one holds only for a limited period the action or process of producing offspring: PROCREATION

the process of coming or bringing into being generation of income

origination by a generating process : PRODUCTION especially : formation of a geometric figure by motion of another

Government (Noun)

The Governing body of a nation, state, or community: "an agency of the federal government"; "government controls" the system by which a nation, state, or community is governed: "a secular, pluralistic, democratic government"

H

Holy (Adjective)

exalted or worthy of complete devotion as one perfect in goodness and righteousness

DIVINE for the Lord our God is *Holy*—Psalms 99:9 (King James Version)

devoted entirely to the deity or the work of the deity a *Holy* temple; *Holy* prophets

having a divine quality *Holy* love

venerated as or as if sacred *Holy* scripture a *Holy* relic

used as an intensive *this is a Holy* mess *he was a Holy* terror when he drank—*Thomas Wolfe* —*often used in combination as a mild oath* Holy smoke

I

Inner Man (Noun)

A man's soul or mind: *"the complexities of the inner man"*

Influence (Noun)

The power or capacity of causing an effect in indirect or intangible SWAY

the act or power of producing an effect without apparent exertion of force or direct exercise of command

corrupt interference with authority for personal gain

one that exerts influence

an emanation of spiritual or moral force

an ethereal fluid held to flow from the stars and to affect the actions of humans

an emanation of occult power held to derive from stars

J

Joy (Noun)

the emotion evoked by well-being, success, or good fortune or by the prospect of possessing what one desires: DELIGHT

the expression or exhibition of such emotion : GAIETY

a state of happiness or felicity: BLISS

a source or cause of delight

K

Kindness (Noun)

the quality or state of being kind; treating people with kindness and respect

a kind deed: FAVOR they did me a great kindness.

archaic: AFFECTION

L

Listen (Verb)

to pay attention to sound listen to music

to hear something with thoughtful attention: give consideration listen to a plea

to be alert to catch an expected sound

Lost (adjective)

not made use of, won, or claimed a *lost* opportunity

no longer possessed a *lost* reputation

no longer known a *lost* tunnel

ruined or destroyed physically or morally: **DESPERATE** a *lost* soul;

M

Manifest (Adjective)

readily perceived by the senses and especially by the sense of sight their sadness was manifest in their faces.

easily understood or recognized by the mind: OBVIOUS manifestly adverb

Mind (Noun)

Recollection, memory

The element or complex (see complex entry 1 sense 1) of elements in an individual that feels, perceives, thinks, wills, and especially reasons the conscious mental events and capabilities in an organism

O

Obedience (Noun)

an act or instance of obeying

the quality or state of being <u>obedient</u> Children should learn *obedience* and respect for authority.

P

Physical (Adjective)

of or relating to natural science

of or relating to physics

characterized or produced by the forces and operations of physics

having material existence: perceptible especially through the senses and subject to the laws of nature.

Physiological (Adjective)

Relating to the branch of biology that deals with the normal functions of living organisms and their parts:

Platform (noun)

a flat horizontal surface that is usually higher than the adjoining area: such as

a raised flooring (such as a stage or dais).

Pollute (verb)

to make ceremonially or morally impure: DEFILE

To make physically impure or unclean: BEFOUL, DIRTY.

R

Rebuke (Verb)

to criticize sharply: REPRIMAND

to serve as a rebuke to

archaic: to turn back or keep down: CHECK

Respect (Noun)

a relation or reference to a particular thing or situation remarks having respect to an earlier plan an act of giving particular attention: CONSIDERATION

high or special regard: ESTEEM

the quality or state of being esteemed

respects plural: expressions of high or special regard or deference paid our respects

S

Safety-harness (Noun)

Safety harnesses: (plural noun), a system of belts or restraints to hold a person to prevent falling or injury.

Sanctification (Noun)

an act of sanctifying

the state of being sanctified

the state of growing in divine grace as a result of Christian commitment after baptism or conversion

Scaffold; (Noun)

a temporary or movable platform for workers (such as bricklayers, painters, or miners) to stand or sit on when working at a height above the floor or ground

a platform on which a criminal is executed (as by hanging or beheading)

a platform at a height above ground or floor level

a supporting framework.

Self-esteem (Noun)

a confidence and satisfaction in oneself: **SELF-RESPECT**

Self-Conceit

Confidence in one's own worth or abilities; self-respect: "assertiveness training for those with low self-esteem.

Self-inflicted (Adjective)

Inflicted or caused by oneself a *self-inflicted* wound

His staff problems are *self-inflicted*, the product of his poor judgment and bad choices. —*The Guardian* (United Kingdom).

Self-government (Noun)

SELF-CONTROL, SELF-COMMAND

government under the control and direction of the inhabitants of a political unit rather than by an outside authority broadly: control of one's own affairs.

Soul (Noun)

The spiritual or immaterial part of a human being or animal, regarded as immortal: bad choices. —*The Guardian* (United Kingdom).

Surrendered (Verb)

To yield to the power, control, or possession of another upon compulsion cease resistance to an enemy or opponent and submit to their authority:

T

Thankful (Adjective)

Pleased and relieved: "they were thankful that the war was finally over" · "I was very thankful to be alive" expressing gratitude and relief.

Transgression (Noun)

An act that goes against a law, rule, or code of conduct; an offense: an act, process, or instance of transgressing: such as: Infringement or violation of a law, command, or duty.

Trust (Noun)

Firm belief in the reliability, truth, ability, or strength of someone or something. Relations have to be built on trust.

U

Unhealthy (Adjective)

not conducive to health: not healthful an unhealthy climate unhealthy habits unhealthy food

not in good health: SICKLY, DISEASED unhealthy animals

Understanding (Noun)

The ability to understand something; comprehension.

Unity (Noun)

The state of being united or joined as a whole.

V

Vessel (Noun)

Any kind of container or receptacle is earthenware. But vessels of glass, metal, leather, wicker, and stone were not uncommon. They were used to hold everything from documents.

Illustrated Dictionary of the Bible / Herbert Lockyer, Sr., Editor / with F.F. Bruce and R.K. Harrison

Vitality (Noun)

The state of being strong and active; energy changes that will give renewed vitality to our democracy.

W

Well-being (Noun)

The state of being happy, healthy, or prosperous: WELFARE

Will (Verb)

Expressing the future tense: "You'll lament it once you are more seasoned" expressing inevitable events: Used to express desire, choice, willingness, consent, or in negative constructions refusal.

Wisdom (Noun)

ability to discern inner qualities and relationships: INSIGHT

Y

Yahweh (Noun)

Yahweh is a name that conveys the thought that God is ever present with his people to save, help, deliver, redeem, bless, and keep covenant

The name YHWH was connected with the Hebrew words 'I am'

God gave no simple explanation of what his name meant, but he reassured his people by stating his name in words that may be translated 'I am who I am' or 'I will be what I will be'

Yahweh is the covenant-keeping name, and it is a subtle promise that God will forever be faithful in keeping his "Bridge-way Bible Dictionary - StudyLight.org"

Yoke (Noun)

a wooden bar or frame by which two draft animals (such as oxen) are joined at the heads or necks for working together

an arched device formerly laid on the neck of a defeated person

a frame fitted to a person's shoulders to carry a load in two equal portions

Plural usually Yoke: two animals <u>yoked</u> or worked together

Z

Zeal (Noun)

great energy or enthusiasm in pursuit of a cause or an objective:

Dictionary Oxford Languages

"his zeal for privatization" · "Laura brought a missionary zeal to her work"

Zion

The city of David and the city of God the meaning of the word Zion underwent a distinct progression in its usage throughout the Bible.

Illustrated Dictionary of the Bible / Herbert Lockyer, Sr., Editor / with F.F. Bruce and R.K. Harrison

Resources

Unless otherwise indicated, all content is licensed under a Creative Commons Attribution License. All Scripture quotations, unless otherwise indicated, are taken from The Holy Bible, English Standard Version. Copyright ©2001 by Crossway Bibles, a publishing ministry of Good News Publishers. Contact me: openbibleinfo (at) gmail.com.

Brokenness

Psalm 34:18 ESV

The Lord is near to the brokenhearted and saves the crushed in spirit.

Psalm 51:17 ESV

The sacrifices of God are a broken spirit; a broken and contrite heart, O God, you will not despise.

Psalm 147:3 ESV

He heals the brokenhearted and binds up their wounds.

Proverbs 3:5-6 ESV

Trust in the Lord with all your heart, and do not lean on your own understanding. In all your ways acknowledge him, and he will make straight your paths.

Isaiah 57:15 ESV

For thus says the One who is high and lifted up, who inhabits eternity, whose name is Holy: "I dwell in the high and Holy place, and also with him who is of a contrite and lowly spirit, to revive the spirit of the lowly, and to revive the heart of the contrite."

John 12:24 ESV

Truly, truly, I say to you, unless a grain of wheat falls into the earth and dies, it remains alone; but if it dies, it bears much fruit.

Psalm 31:12 ESV

I have been forgotten like one who is dead; I have become like a broken vessel.

2 Corinthians 1:8-10 ESV

For we do not want you to be unaware, brothers, of the affliction we experienced in Asia. For we were so utterly burdened beyond our strength that we despaired of life itself. Indeed, we felt that we had received the sentence of death. But that was to make us rely not on ourselves but on God who raises the dead. He delivered us from such a deadly peril, and he will deliver us. On him we have set our hope that he will deliver us again.

Matthew 5:2-12 ESV

And he opened his mouth and taught them, saying: "Blessed are the poor in spirit, for theirs is the Kingdom of heaven. . . .

Blessed are those who mourn, for they shall be comforted. . . . Blessed are the meek, for they shall inherit the earth. . . . Blessed are those who hunger and thirst for righteousness, for they shall be satisfied."

James 4:6 ESV

But he gives more grace. Therefore it says, "God opposes the proud but gives grace to the humble."

Isaiah 66:2 ESV

All these things my hand has made, and so all these things came to be, declares the Lord. But this is the one to whom I will look: he who is humble and contrite in spirit and trembles at my word.

Galatians 2:20 ESV

I have been crucified with Christ. It is no longer I who live, but Christ who lives in me. And the life I now live in the flesh I live by faith in the Son of God, who loved me and gave himself for me.

Jeremiah 18:1-23 ESV

The word that came to Jeremiah from the Lord: "Arise, and go down to the potter's house, and there I will let you hear my words." So I went down to the potter's house, and there he was working at his wheel. And the vessel he was making of clay was spoiled in the potter's hand, and he reworked it into another vessel, as it seemed good to the potter to do. Then the word of the Lord came to me . . .

James 5:16 ESV

Therefore, confess your sins to one another and pray for one another, that you may be healed. The prayer of a righteous person has great power as it is working.

Isaiah 66:1-2 ESV

Thus says the Lord: "Heaven is my throne, and the earth is my footstool; what is the house that you would build for me, and what is the place of my rest? All these things my hand has made, and so all these things came to be, declares the Lord. But this is the one to whom I will look: he who is humble and contrite in spirit and trembles at my word."

Eyes

Matthew 6:22 ESV

"The eye is the lamp of the body. So, if your eye is healthy, your whole body will be full of light."

Psalm 101:3 ESV

I will not set before my eyes anything that is worthless. I hate the work of those who fall away; it shall not cling to me.

1 Samuel 16:7 ESV

But the Lord said to Samuel, "Do not look on his appearance or on the height of his stature, because I have rejected him. For the Lord sees not as man sees: man looks on the outward appearance, but the Lord looks on the heart."

Psalm 119:18 ESV

Open my eyes, that I may behold wondrous things out of your law.

2 Kings 6:17 ESV

Then Elisha prayed and said, "O Lord, please open his eyes that he may see." So the Lord opened the eyes of the young man, and he saw, and behold, the mountain was full of horses and chariots of fire all around Elisha.

Luke 11:33-36 ESV

"No one after lighting a lamp puts it in a cellar or under a basket, but on a stand, so that those who enter may see the light. Your eye is the lamp of your body. When your eye is healthy, your whole body is full of light, but when it is bad, your body is full of darkness. Therefore be careful lest the light in you be darkness. If then your whole body is full of light, having no part dark, it will be wholly bright, as when a lamp with its rays gives you light."

Matthew 5:28 ESV

But I say to you that everyone who looks at a woman with lustful intent has already committed adultery with her in his heart.

Proverbs 20:12 ESV

The hearing ear and the seeing eye, the Lord has made them both.

Mark 8:25 ESV

Then Jesus laid his hands on his eyes again; and he opened his eyes, his sight was restored, and he saw everything clearly.

Matthew 5:29 ESV

If your right eye causes you to sin, tear it out and throw it away. For it is better that you lose one of your members than that your whole body be thrown into hell.

Ephesians 1:16-21 ESV

I do not cease to give thanks for you, remembering you in my prayers, that the God of our Lord Jesus Christ, the Father of glory, may give you the Spirit of wisdom and of revelation in the knowledge of him, having the eyes of your hearts enlightened, that you may know what is the hope to which he has called you, what are the riches of his glorious inheritance in the saints, and what is the immeasurable greatness of his power toward us who believe, according to the working of his great might that he worked in Christ when he raised him from the dead and seated him at his right hand in the heavenly places . . .

Proverbs 21:4 ESV

Haughty eyes and a proud heart, the lamp of the wicked, are sin.

Job 31:7 ESV

If my step has turned aside from the way and my heart has gone after my eyes, and if any spot has stuck to my hands,

Job 31:1 ESV

"I have made a covenant with my eyes; how then could I gaze at a virgin?"

Eye Gates

Psalm 101:3-4 ESV

I will not set before my eyes anything that is worthless. I hate the work of those who fall away; it shall not cling to me. A perverse heart shall be far from me; I will know nothing of evil.

Matthew 5:1-48 ESV

Seeing the crowds, he went up on the mountain, and when he sat down, his disciples came to him. And he opened his mouth and taught them, saying: "Blessed are the poor in spirit, for theirs is the Kingdom of heaven. . . . Blessed are those who mourn, for they shall be comforted. . . . Blessed are the meek, for they shall inherit the earth."

Hebrews 4:12 ESV

For the word of God is living and active, sharper than any two-edged sword, piercing to the division of soul and of spirit, of joints and of marrow, and discerning the thoughts and intentions of the heart.

Philippians 4:8 ESV

Finally, brothers, whatever is true, whatever is honorable, whatever is just, whatever is pure, whatever is lovely, whatever is commendable, if there is any excellence, if there is anything worthy of praise, think about these things.

1 Corinthians 13:1–13 ESV

If I speak in the tongues of men and of angels, but have not love, I am a noisy gong or a clanging cymbal. And if I have prophetic powers, and understand all mysteries and all knowledge, and if I have all faith, so as to remove mountains, but have not love, I am nothing. If I give away all I have, and if I deliver up my body to be burned, but have not love, I gain nothing. Love is patient and kind; love does not envy or boast; it is not arrogant or rude. It does not insist on its own way; it is not irritable or resentful . . .

Mark 4:24 ESV

And he said to them, "Pay attention to what you hear: with the measure you use, it will be measured to you, and still more will be added to you."

Ezekiel 20:7 ESV

And I said to them, 'Cast away the detestable things your eyes feast on, every one of you, and do not defile yourselves with the idols of Egypt; I am the Lord your God.'

Philippians 4:8 ESV

Finally, brothers, whatever is true, whatever is honorable, whatever is just, whatever is pure, whatever is lovely, whatever is commendable, if there is any excellence, if there is anything worthy of praise, think about these things.

Romans 12:2 ESV

Do not be conformed to this world, but be transformed by the renewal of your mind, that by testing you may discern what is the will of God, what is good and acceptable and perfect.

2 Corinthians 10:5 ESV

We destroy arguments and every lofty opinion raised against the knowledge of God, and take every thought captive to obey Christ,

Isaiah 26:3 ESV

You keep him in perfect peace whose mind is stayed on you, because he trusts in you.

Proverbs 4:23 ESV

Keep your heart with all vigilance, for from it flow the springs of life.

1 Corinthians 1:10 ESV

I appeal to you, brothers, by the name of our Lord Jesus Christ, that all of you agree, and that there be no divisions among you, but that you be united in the same mind and the same judgment.

Isaiah 55:8-9 ESV

For my thoughts are not your thoughts, neither are your ways my ways, declares the Lord. For as the heavens are higher than the earth, so are my ways higher than your ways and my thoughts than your thoughts.

Hebrews 4:12 ESV

For the word of God is living and active, sharper than any two-edged sword, piercing to the division of soul and of spirit, of joints and of marrow, and discerning the thoughts and intentions of the heart.

Mark 7:20-23 ESV

And he said, "What comes out of a person is what defiles him. For from within, out of the heart of man, come evil thoughts, sexual immorality, theft, murder, adultery, coveting, wickedness, deceit, sensuality, envy, slander, pride, foolishness. All these evil things come from within, and they defile a person."

Jeremiah 29:11 ESV

For I know the plans I have for you, declares the Lord, plans for welfare and not for evil, to give you a future and a hope.

Matthew 21:22 ESV

And whatever you ask in prayer, you will receive, if you have faith."

2 Timothy 1:7 ESV

For God gave us a spirit not of fear but of power and love and self-control.

Colossians 3:1-2 ESV

If then you have been raised with Christ, seek the things that are above, where Christ is, seated at the right hand of God. Set your minds on things that are above, not on things that are on earth.

Romans 7:23 ESV

But I see in my members another law waging war against the law of my mind and making me captive to the law of sin that dwells in my members.

Image

Genesis 1:27 ESV

So God created man in his own image, in the image of God he created him; male and female he created them.

Genesis 1:26 ESV

Then God said, "Let us make man in our image, after our likeness. And let them have dominion over the fish of the sea and over the birds of the heavens and over the livestock and over all the earth and over every creeping thing that creeps on the earth."

Ephesians 4:24 ESV

And to put on the new self, created after the likeness of God in true righteousness and holiness.

Genesis 1:26-27 ESV

Then God said, "Let us make man in our image, after our likeness. And let them have dominion over the fish of the sea and over the birds of the heavens and over the livestock and over all the earth and over every creeping thing that creeps on the earth." So God created man in his own image, in the image of God he created him; male and female he created them.

2 Corinthians 3:18 ESV

And we all, with unveiled face, beholding the glory of the Lord, are being transformed into the same image from one degree of glory to another, For this comes from the Lord who is the Spirit.

Colossians 3:10 ESV

And have put on the new self, which is being renewed in knowledge after the image of its creator.

Psalm 17:15 ESV

As for me, I shall behold your face in righteousness; when I awake, I shall be satisfied with your likeness.

Philippians 2:3 ESV

Do nothing from selfish ambition or conceit, but in humility count others more significant than yourselves.

2 Timothy 3:2 ESV

For people will be lovers of self, lovers of money, proud, arrogant, abusive, disobedient to their parents, ungrateful, unholy,

Temptation

1 Corinthians 10:13 ESV

No temptation has overtaken you that is not common to man. God is faithful, and he will not let you be tempted beyond your ability, but with the temptation he will also provide the way of escape, that you may be able to endure it.

Matthew 26:41 ESV

Watch and pray that you may not enter into temptation. The spirit indeed is willing, but the flesh is weak."

James 4:7 ESV

Submit yourselves therefore to God. Resist the devil, and he will flee from you.

James 1:12-16 ESV

Blessed is the man who remains steadfast under trial, for when he has stood the test he will receive the crown of life, which God has promised to those who love him. Let no one say when he is tempted, "I am being tempted by God," for God cannot be tempted with evil, and he himself tempts no one. But each person is tempted when he is lured and enticed by his own desire. Then desire when it has conceived gives birth to sin, and sin when it is fully grown brings forth death. Do not be deceived, my beloved brothers.

Hebrews 2:18 ESV

For because he himself has suffered when tempted, he is able to help those who are being tempted.

Ephesians 6:11 ESV

Put on the whole armor of God that you may be able to stand against the schemes of the devil.

Resources

Matthew 4:1-11 ESV

Then Jesus was led up by the Spirit into the wilderness to be tempted by the devil. And after fasting forty days and forty nights, he was hungry. And the tempter came and said to him, "If you are the Son of God, command these stones to become loaves of bread." But he answered, "It is written, "'Man shall not live by bread alone, but by every word that comes from the mouth of God.'" Then the devil took him to the Holy City and set him to the pinnacle of the temple . . .

Mark 14:38 ESV

Watch and pray that you may not enter into temptation. The spirit indeed is willing, but the flesh is weak."

Ephesians 4:27 ESV

And give no opportunity to the devil.

James 1:12 ESV

Blessed is the man who remains steadfast under trial, for when he has stood the test he will receive the crown of life, which God has promised to those who love him.

1 Timothy 5:8 ESV

But if anyone does not provide for his relatives, and especially for members of his household, he has denied the faith and is worse than an unbeliever.

Ephesians 4:28 ESV

Let the thief no longer steal, but rather let him labor, doing honest work with his own hands, so that he may have something to share with anyone in need.

Acts 20:35 ESV

In all things I have shown you that by working hard in this way we must help the weak and remember the words of the Lord Jesus, how he himself said, 'It is more blessed to give than to receive.'"

Proverbs 14:23 ESV

In all toil there is profit, but mere talk tends only to poverty.

Genesis 2:15 ESV

The Lord God took the man and put him in the Garden of Eden to work it and keep it.

Colossians 3:23 ESV

Whatever you do, work heartily, as for the Lord and not for men,

Luke 10:7 ESV

And remain in the same house, eating and drinking what they provide, for the laborer deserves his wages. Do not go from house to house.

Ecclesiastes 9:10 ESV

Whatever your hand finds to do, do it with your might, for there is no work or thought or knowledge or wisdom in Sheol, to which you are going.

Proverbs 18:9 ESV

Whoever is slack in his work is a brother to him who destroys.

Proverbs 13:4 ESV

The soul of the sluggard craves and gets nothing, while the soul of the diligent is richly supplied.

Commit Exercise

It is imperative to cultivate one's faith and conscientiously self-assess one's language, as this practice serves as an expression of one's innermost beliefs and has the potential to uplift both oneself and others. Engaging in this process is essential for the preservation of one's integrity and self-image and necessitates regular, daily reflection. The linguistic choices utilized in positive communication have a substantial influence on the comprehension of a message. The improper utilization of language by a speaker has the potential to result in misunderstandings and ineffective communication.

Commit Exercise

Words that are practical and accomplishable Uttering words that hold no ethical or moral value.

Build yourself up on a daily basis and feed your spirit with great words.

Positive Value Exercise

The values that you possess in your life reflect what is important to you. Understanding your values can have a significant impact on identifying what motivates you, what you value, what sparks your inspiration, and what you desire more of in life. Here is a compilation of words that can be used to shape a lifestyle that reflects our core beliefs. We have the capability to create a meaningful and significant life for ourselves. As time goes by, values revolve and expand as you gain a deeper understanding of yourself. They are in constant motion. We all have unique qualities, so undoubtedly, there will be some words missing from this list that should be added. Pick a few to reflect and meditate on, as this will aid in transforming your mindset.

Positive Value Exercise

1. Accomplishment
2. Accuracy
3. Acknowledgment
4. Adventure
5. Authenticity
6. Balance
7. Beauty
8. Boldness
9. Calm
10. Challenge
11. Collaboration
12. Community
13. Compassion
14. Comradeship
15. Confidence
16. Connectedness
17. Contentment
18. Contribution
19. Cooperation
20. Courage
21. Creativity
22. Curiosity
23. Determination
24. Directness
25. Discovery
26. Ease
27. Effortlessness
28. Empowerment
29. Enthusiasm
30. Environment
31. Excellence
32. Fairness
33. Flexibility
34. Focus
35. Forgiveness
36. Freedom
37. Friendship
38. Fun
39. Generosity
40. Gentleness
41. Growth
42. Happiness
43. Harmony
44. Health
45. Helpfulness
46. Honesty
47. Honor
48. Humor
49. Idealism
50. Independence
51. Innovation
52. Integrity
53. Intuition
54. Joy
55. Kindness
56. Learning
57. Listening
58. Love
59. Loyalty
60. Optimism
61. Orderliness
62. Participation
63. Partnership
64. Passion
65. Patience
66. Peace
67. Presence
68. Productivity
69. Recognition
70. Respect
71. Resourcefulness
72. Romance
73. Safety
74. Self-Esteem
75. Service
76. Simplicity
77. Spaciousness
78. Spirituality
79. Spontaneity
80. Strength
81. Tact
82. Thankfulness
83. Tolerance
84. Tradition
85. Trust
86. Understanding
87. Unity
88. Vitality
89. Wisdom
90. _____
91. _____
92. _____
93. _____
94. _____
95. _____
96. _____
97. _____
98. _____
99. _____

Resources for Young Men Growing in Faith

During a mentoring session, a mentee posed a question regarding the significance of standing firm in the covenant of true belief of God. I asked where he found his strength and happiness, whether it came from within himself or from God's kindness. I stressed the importance of the heart in supporting and maintaining spiritual health, emphasizing the importance of showing this dedication through one's actions. Therefore, it is clear that there are multiple elements of stewardship that can be successfully applied based on this comprehension.

- A young man has to stand firm on being empowered by his father or male figure.
- A young man has to stand firm on being accommodated to God's Word.
- A young man must stand and observe his visual recognition daily from the enemy, who brings the desire to his vision.
- A young man needs to stand on supplication day by day.
- A young man has to stand firm in examining God's Word daily.
- A young man needs to stand on learning unused words and being around positive individuals.
- A young man has to stand firm on repenting.

- A young man must stand firm on respecting others and himself.
- A young man must stand firm on creating a positive choice.
- A young man has to stand firm on hearing the voice of God in his life.
- A young man has to stand firm on his targets and dreams.
- A young man has to stand firm on how to supervise his issues.
- A young man has to stand firm and spend time alone with himself.

For More Resources

Blog: www.letsbreakbreadwith.wixsite.com/website-1

www.letsbreakbreadcoach.com

- The Dimension in Covenant
- Sober-Minded
- Double Agent
- The Power of Your Authority
- Effective Communication
- Spotlight on Integrity

Pod Cast: Podbean

- Personal Leadership
- True Character Has a Place
- His Voice Is in Integrity

YouTube: Let's Break Bread Fathering and Mentoring Program

- www.youtubecom/letmichaelbread

For More Resources

Artwork by Glenn Rodriguez

Surrender | Definition of surrender by Merriam-Webster. http://merriam-webstercollegiate.com/dictionary/surrender

New International Version (NIV)

Holy Bible, New International Version®, NIV® Copyright ©1973, 1978, 1984, 2011 by Biblical, Inc.® Used by permission. All rights reserved worldwide.

The Kingdom of God is righteousness peace and joy (NIV). https://precisiongraphics.com/8581ax/the-kingdom-of-god-is-righteousness-peace-and-joy-niv-bb1c8c **Romans 14:17 New International Version (NIV)**

New Living Translation (NLT)

Holy Bible, New Living Translation, copyright © 1996, 2004, 2015 by Tyndale House Foundation. Used by permission of Tyndale House Publishers, Inc., Carol Stream, Illinois 60188. All rights reserved.

New American Standard Bible (NASB)

New American Standard Bible®, Copyright © 1960, 1971, 1977, 1995, 2020 by The Lockman Foundation. All rights reserved.

Bible Pathway Ministries

Bible Pathways 03/23/2004 - Daily Devotional. https://www.crosswalk.com/devotionals/biblepathways/bible-pathways-03-or-23-or-2004-1249415.html

Pursuing Wholeness - A spiritual guide for the broken | Azanishelise.com. https://azanishelise.com/pursuing-wholeness/

For More Resources

21st Century King James Version (Kj21)

The Holy Bible, 21st Century King James Version® (KJ21®) Copyright ©1994 by Deuel Enterprises, Inc., Gary, SD 57237. All rights reserved.

Scripture quotations taken from the 21st Century King James Version®, copyright © 1994. Used by permission of Deuel Enterprises, Inc., Gary, SD 57237. All rights reserved.

Notwithstanding the above, short quotations from the KJ21 may be used without written permission for noncommercial purposes, such as church bulletins, orders of service, posters, transparencies, etc., with the designation *KJ21*® affixed at the end thereof, and for brief quotations in book reviews and articles.

Quotations in excess of two hundred (200) verses or 40 percent of the work in which they are quoted, or other permission requests, must be directed to and approved in writing by Deuel Enterprises, Inc., PO Box 40, Gary, SD 57237.

Publication of any commentary or other Bible reference work produced for commercial sale that uses the 21st Century King James Version text requires written permission.

Unless otherwise indicated, all content is licensed under a Creative Commons Attribution License. All Scripture quotations, unless otherwise indicated, are taken from The Holy Bible, English Standard Version. Copyright ©2001 by Crossway Bibles, a publishing ministry of Good News Publishers. Contact me: openbibleinfo (at) gmail.com.

Author's Bio

Michael Turner has been in leadership and life coaching for over twenty-five years. He has a certificate in Christian counseling from the American Association of Christian Counseling, and he has helped establish a Christian counseling service.

Michael's professional career spans working with special education disability participants, managing over 200 employees in a Fortune 500 Company, and serving as a youth leader for over ten years with Harvest Christian Center. Michael created Commander Classes to help men become more like Christ, and he devotes his time to caring for God's people by serving those in the greatest need and bringing them to salvation.

www.ingramcontent.com/pod-product-compliance
Lightning Source LLC
LaVergne TN
LVHW011852060526
838200LV00054B/4290